Little Madison and the Day Maple Hollow Disagreed

A Coloring Story About Finding Common Ground

For young thinkers learning to share the square

By David Page

Warped Minds Press

This Book Belongs To:

____

A proud citizen of Maple Hollow.

When everyone shouts, no one is heard.

Taking turns helps everyone speak.

Stubborn feet stop everyone.

Sometimes stepping back moves us forward.

Big ideas need teamwork.

Rules help us work together.

Quiet minds grow strong ideas.

Strong voices are good. Listening is better.

When we cannot agree, we vote.

Even when we lose, we still belong.

Problems are easier when we fix them together.

Small voices matter too.

Fair leaders follow the rules too.

Fair shares make happy neighbors.

Saying sorry makes strong friends.

Many hands build strong bridges.

Listening brings us closer.

Sometimes the best idea is a new idea.

Together, we cross to the other side.

When we listen and work together, everyone belongs.